to June
with very best
wishes from GEOFFREY. Xmas 1936.

OUR PRINCESSES
AND THEIR DOGS

OUR PRINCESSES

AND THEIR DOGS

By

MICHAEL CHANCE

PHOTOGRAPHS BY
STUDIO LISA

LONDON
JOHN MURRAY, ALBEMARLE STREET, W

First Edition 1936

*Printed in Great Britain by Messrs. Bemrose & Sons Ltd.,
Derby, and bound by Messrs. Butler & Tanner, Ltd., Frome.*

TO ALL CHILDREN WHO LOVE DOGS

FOREWORD

IT is no mere conventional courtesy but the plain truth that urges me to say that Princess Elizabeth and Princess Margaret Rose, together with their parents the Duke and Duchess of York, are not only deeply attached to their dogs, but—which is far more important in a dog's eyes—possess an unusual gift for understanding their animals.

All the world knows that in their relations with those with whom they come in contact our Princesses reveal a simplicity worthy of their House, a graciousness that is all their own: which is only another way of saying that had they been commoners they would still stand out from others as children of uncommon charm. But few people realise the marked similarity between the unaffected sincerity that so delightfully characterises these Royal but very human children and the cheerful contentment of their dogs.

Accustomed as I am to meeting every kind of dog in the company of all kinds of masters and mistresses, I doubt if I have ever encountered dogs who shared with their owners a quieter or serener companionship. In other words, our Princesses and their dogs are true friends together. Which, indeed, should be the relationship between all children and their pets.

Because Her Royal Highness the Duchess of York warmly subscribes to this view, it is doubly gratifying that Her Royal Highness should herself have graciously suggested that this book should be dedicated " To All Children Who Love Dogs." No dedication could be simpler, none more impressive.

Those who have been privileged to be received at Royal Lodge, Windsor Great Park, the country home near London where the Duke and Duchess of York and their children find their pleasantest relaxation from the relentless, crowded hours of official duties, have good reason to know the truth of the statement that our British Royalty is most royal in its simplicity. And Royal Lodge itself, an unpretentious, charmingly proportioned white house tucked away in a quiet green corner of Windsor Great Park, is as unselfconscious and devoid of artificiality as are its owners.

Here is the garden whose planning and development has given such pleasure to that enthusiastic gardener the Duchess of York, a garden that in Spring is brilliantly gay with wisteria, azaleas, tulips, laburnum trees, rhododendrons, lilac, and a riot of other colourful flowers beloved of its creator. Here, too, in the rose garden stands Princess Elizabeth's proud little house that was given to her by the people of Wales on her sixth birthday, and is still cared for and kept spick and span by no one but the Princesses themselves.

Here, also, are to be found the eight dogs that are the present companions of our Princesses, cheerful yet well trained dogs whose general gaiety of spirit is clear testimony to the affection and care bestowed upon each animal.

First in importance, since they are essentially the property and constant companions of the two Princesses, come the two Pembrokeshire Corgis, the three-and-a-half year old Dookie (Golden Eagle), and the eighteen months old Jane (Lady Jane). These two reddish-brown little dogs (Jane is slightly darker in colour than Dookie) are not only deeply attached to their young mistresses and each other, but enjoy life with a zest that is good to see. They evidently, and very properly, believe that whatever is worth doing is worth enjoying. Amongst their amusements may be mentioned interminable games of hide and seek with each other, and that still greater game of jumping over either of their mistresses whenever the opportunity occurs.

Gay, active, intelligent and faithful little creatures are Dookie and Jane.

The three well-bred Yellow Labradors, Mimsy and her son and daughter, Stiffy and Scrummy, are primarily the property of the Duke of York, but they are an essential part of the entire canine family that romps with the Princesses when they are at Royal Lodge. Moreover, it is clear that the two younger Labradors have inherited the gentle good nature of their mother.

Outwardly the most interesting of all the dogs is possibly the long-haired grey and white Tibetan Lion Dog Choo-Choo, as Oriental in character as he is in ancestry; for no matter how the other dogs may group themselves or on what business they may be engaged, the picturesque Choo-Choo invariably decides on isolated splendour.

There are also Judy, a six-year old Golden Retriever, and Ben, a black Cocker Spaniel of the same age. All these dogs live together on terms of perfect amity, if one excepts the occasional tendency of Dookie to disturb the harmony of the scene by his somewhat arrogant but none the less lovably amusing attempts to impose his will on Choo-Choo or, for that matter, on any of the other dogs who may be so foolhardy as to arouse his ire. Dookie, in other words, is the " character " of the party, and as such is the avowed favourite of Princess Elizabeth and her mother.

Nevertheless, as is stated elsewhere, the two Princesses, their parents *and* their dogs constitute one very human and happy family.

It is not surprising that our popular Princesses should continually be offered dogs of every size and shape by people anxious to further the claims of the particular breed in which they are interested, the number of dogs so offered running into many hundreds in the course of a year. But the Princesses remain true to their Labradors and Corgis, the faithful yet sporting instincts of both breeds (Corgis having long been known as the little cattle dogs of Wales) ensuring their continued popularity in this particular household.

It is good to be able to record the fact that our Princesses and their parents are not merely dog owners but are essentially dog lovers. That is to say, owners who not only love their dogs but show them consideration as well. Owners who make their dogs happy . . . Too many dogs potter through life, with little to amuse them between one meal-time and another.

But Dookie, Jane and the others lead a grand existence. What more can a dog want than that his two mistresses should also be his friends and companions ? Moreover, just as we humans know that in all the world there are no Royalties so unselfconscious as our own, none so considerate of others, so devoid of artificiality, so rich in human qualities, it may well be that Dookie and Jane, being dogs of sense, instinctively share our knowledge.

At any rate, it is precisely these characteristics in a mistress that bring home to a dog the real meaning of the word happiness.

A delightful tulip-time picture of the Pembrokeshire Welsh Corgi, Jane (registered as Lady Jane), lying blissfully between her happy young mistresses, Princess Elizabeth and Princess Margaret Rose. In most of the photographs that follow, the eighteen months old Jane is distinguishable from the three-and-a-half year old Dookie by reason of her darker mask.

In this charmingly informal group, Choo-Choo, the Tibetan Lion Dog, is accepting adulation from the Duke of York and Princess Margaret Rose with typically Oriental detachment.

While the Welsh Corgi, Dookie (registered as Golden Eagle), averts his eyes in disgusted jealousy, there is no mistaking the deep affection with which Mimsy, the Duke of York's favourite Yellow Labrador, is regarding her Royal master.

Jane and Dookie, very much alert as they watch a mysterious movement amongst the rhododendrons, share a seat with Princess Elizabeth in the garden of the Duke of York's London house. Dookie, well aware that of all his companions he is the avowed favourite of both the Duchess of York and Princess Elizabeth, has insisted on occupying the place of honour nearest to his mistress.

The two dogs in the foreground—particularly Jane—seem proudly conscious of the fact that the radiance of the Duchess of York and the sunny smiles of the Princesses are a joy to everyone throughout the length and breadth of Britain.

Princess Margaret Rose, kilted and smiling, holds up for inspection the attractive woolly mat known as Choo-Choo. Choo-Choo, it should be explained, was thus named by the Duchess of York because on his first arrival he amused everyone by puffing and scurrying across the lawn for all the world like a train in a hurry.

Nevertheless, Choo-Choo is not Princess Margaret Rose's favourite. Nor is Dookie, nor Jane, nor Mimsy, nor Stiffy, nor Scrummy, nor Judy, nor Ben. Asked which of the dogs she liked best, the little Princess gave deliberate consideration to her reply. " I love them all the same" at length came the emphatic and diplomatic answer. Perhaps, after all, that is how dogs should be loved.

The reality of the Duke of York's sustained interest in his dogs, particularly his Yellow Labradors, is unmistakable.

Here, the six-year old Mimsy, the Duke's favourite Labrador, makes it very clear that her master inspires in his dogs a devotion far stronger than the conventional love of most domestic animals.

" It may be an upside-down world" says Jane, " but I wouldn't change places with any Corgi alive."   Dookie says nothing but looks a lot.

Two Princesses and two Corgis say " How d'you do ? " as they look out of the kitchen windows of the little thatched house that was presented by the people of Wales to Princess Elizabeth on her sixth birthday. This little house is a constant source of pride to its owner. A fairy house that is a real house—" MY house," as Princess Elizabeth emphatically calls it. Moreover, it is entirely cared for and kept spick and span by the Princesses themselves, true mistresses of their own domain.

Devoted as they are to the Duchess of York and the Princesses, it is easy to see that all the dogs acknowledge the Duke of York as their master. Let the Duke move away from one corner of the garden to another and every dog will automatically follow him; and not all the blandishments of their young mistresses can persuade one of them to leave its master.

Biscuit-time in one of the tree-studded corners of Windsor Great Park adjoining the garden of Royal Lodge.

Here one receives—and rightly so—the clear impression that the Duke and Duchess of York, the two Princesses and all their dogs constitute one very human family.

It is precisely this atmosphere of quiet but unmistakable happiness, as conveyed by each animal, that is the hall-mark of real companionship between dogs and their owners.

From one of the windows of her little Welsh house, Princess Elizabeth appropriately introduces one of her Welsh Corgis to her father's Yellow Labrador, Mimsy, who is as affectionate in character as she is handsome in appearance.

Partly because of their more convenient size, it is Dookie and Jane who see most of the world with their young mistresses, not only accompanying them to the London house and wandering at will through its handsome rooms, but travelling everywhere with them on visits to relatives or friends.

Dookie is unquestionably the " character " of the Princesses' delightful canine family.   Although inclined to occasional but harmless truculence—the unfortunate Choo-Choo bearing the brunt of most of his rumbling insults—it would seem from this picture that he is also a born sentimentalist.

It is easy to understand the enthusiasm of the Duke of York, himself a keen and accomplished shot, for his three Yellow Labradors, Mimsy and her son and daughter, Stiffy and Scrummy.

Mimsy is by the famous Golden Morn ex Knaith Bonnet, and deep is the Duke's regret that, after presenting him four years ago with Stiffy and Scrummy, she has so far failed to breed further litters. The sire of Stiffy and his sister was Jock, a grandson of the well-known dog Belvoir Bever.

No more delightful out-of-door picture than this can ever have been taken of Princess Margaret Rose.

If to the Duke and Duchess of York it is a matter for pride that their children possess such charming natures and such sunny smiles, it must equally be a matter of deep satisfaction to the dogs. For a dog owes more happiness in life than most of us realise to precisely those two assets—its mistress's consideration and its mistress's smile.

Who says " No tit-bits " ? Jane has never heard such nonsense in her life.

It is rude of Dookie to look so bored, but as he is two years older than Jane it may be that he considers such behaviour establishes his superiority. Dookie, it must be remembered, is over three years old!

An idyllic picture of two happy little ladies surrounded by five dogs who combine obedience with independence to a remarkable degree.

The dogs were quietly told to lie down, and without hesitation automatically posed themselves round their mistresses in this fashion.

Judging by Jane's expression, it is possible that the joke, obviously thoroughly enjoyed by the Princesses and Dookie, was at her expense.

But Corgis could not through the ages have been brave and efficient little cattle-dogs, guarding flocks and crops single-handed, had they not also been philosophers.

The Duchess of York and the Princesses take a personal pride in the care and grooming of their own dogs. The dogs, being owned by real dog lovers, are not regarded as mere chattels but as living and beloved creatures to be cherished with that individual care and practical help without which affection is but an empty word.

Small wonder that these particular dogs, by the very gaiety of their demeanour, show that they find life vastly worth the living.

This picture should make a strong appeal to every dog lover. Here, clearly, is a man who strikes a personal note with his animals, and who receives in return a faith and friendship that honours equally both man and dog.

Royal dog-lovers standing on the terrace overlooking the garden of their Piccadilly house . . . not merely people who love dogs but warm-hearted, human people who, understanding their animals, are therefore understood by them in return.

It is such people, not those who love their dogs largely for their own gratification, who are the real dog lovers of this world.

This affords an admirable impression of Princess Elizabeth's miniature Welsh house as it stands serenely in the rose garden of Royal Lodge. Elegantly timbered and thatched, Y Bwthyn Bach (The Little House) boasts six rooms, unlimited hot and cold water and a wireless set; but, incredible thought, there is no telephone!

Many are the days spent by the dogs in this house as they watch their young mistresses busying themselves with its practical appliances, and conscientiously leaving no trace of untidiness behind them. For whatever their occupation of the moment may be, our Princesses and their dogs are at all times the best of good companions together.